My Favorite Sports

I LOVE HOCKEY

By Ryan Nagelhout

Gareth Stevens
PUBLISHING

Please visit our website, www.garethstevens.com. For a free color catalog of all our high-quality books, call toll free 1-800-542-2595 or fax 1-877-542-2596.

Library of Congress Cataloging-in-Publication Data

Nagelhout, Ryan.
I love hockey / by Ryan Nagelhout.
p. cm. — (My favorite sports)
Includes index.
ISBN 978-1-4824-0732-7 (pbk.)
ISBN 978-1-4824-0771-6 (6-pack)
ISBN 978-1-4824-0731-0 (library binding)
1. Hockey — Juvenile literature. I. Nagelhout, Ryan. II. Title.
GV847.25 N34 2015
796.962—d23

First Edition

Published in 2015 by
Gareth Stevens Publishing
111 East 14th Street, Suite 349
New York, NY 10003

Editor: Ryan Nagelhout
Designer: Nick Domiano

Photo credits: Cover, pp. 1, 7, 9, 17, 19 Lorraine Swanson/Shuttertstock.com; p. 5 Thomas Barwick/Iconica/ Getty Images; p. 9 Jupiter Images/Thinkstock.com; pp. 11/ 24 (ice skates) Victor Martello/iStock/Thinkstock.com; pp. 13, 24 (stick) Stockbyte/Thinkstock.com; p. 15 bigjohn36/iStock/Thinkstock.com; pp. 21, 24 (puck) Vaclav Volrab/Shutterstock.com; p. 23 (kids) Aptyp_koK/Shutterstock.com; p. 23 (gym background) photobank.ch/ Shutterstock.com.

Printed in the United States of America

CPSIA compliance information: Batch #CS15GS: For further information contact Gareth Stevens, New York, New York at 1-800-542-2595.

Contents

Hockey is
my favorite sport.

5

I play on a team.

We play on ice.

I get to wear ice skates.

I use a stick.

My stick is made from wood.

15

I play with my friends.

17

We love to pass
the puck.

It is made of rubber.

I also like to play floor hockey.

Words to Know

ice skates   puck   stick

Index